Play with Shapes!

by Mary Alice Cooper

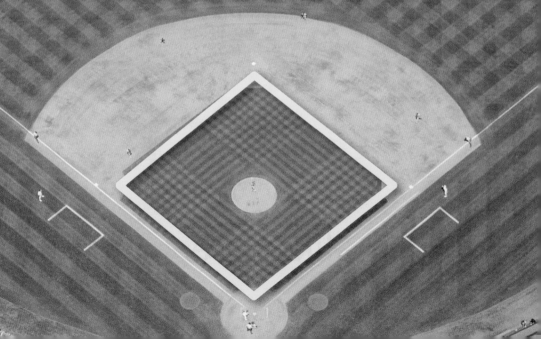

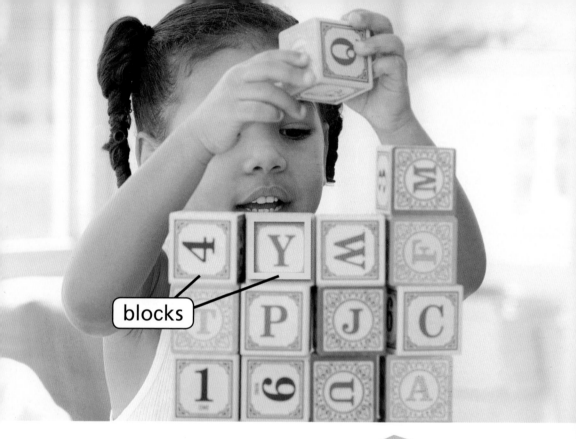

blocks

We like the .

blocks

2

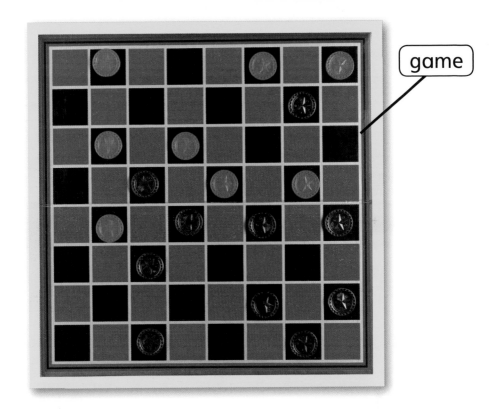

game

We like the 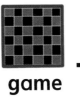 .

game

3

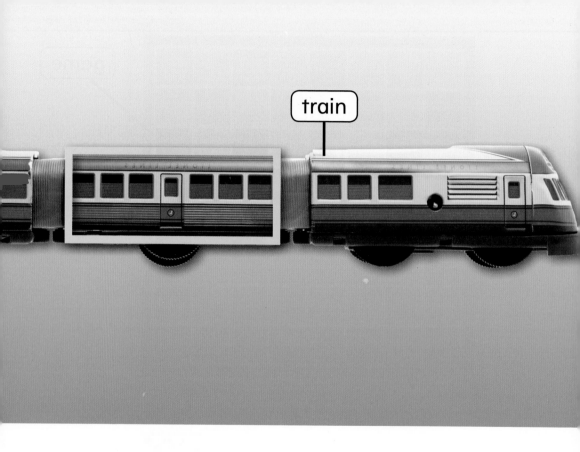

train

We like the .

train

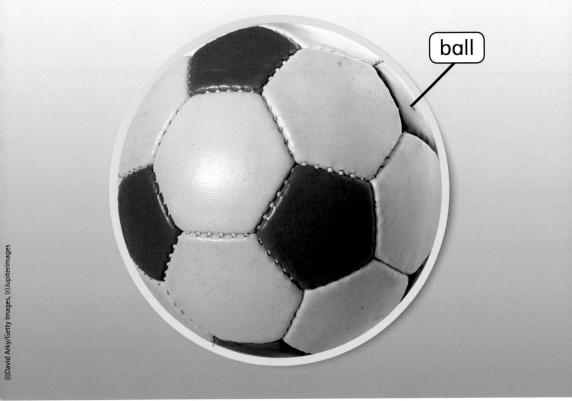

ball

We like the ball.

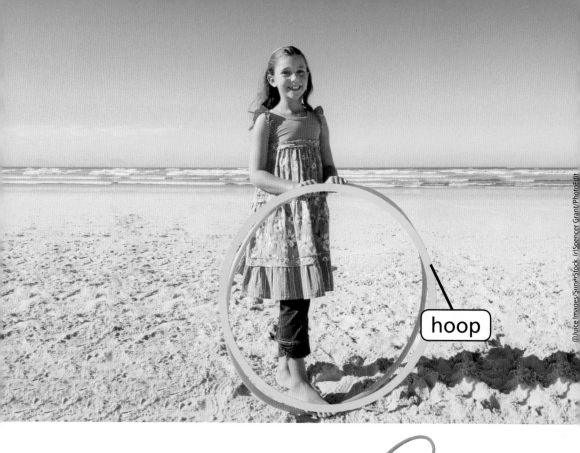

hoop

We like the ◯.
hoop

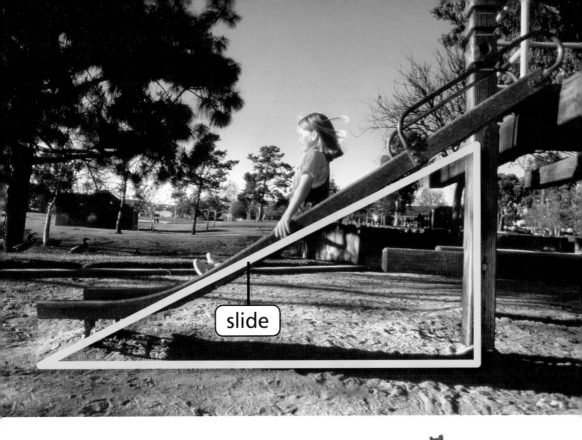

slide

We like the .

slide

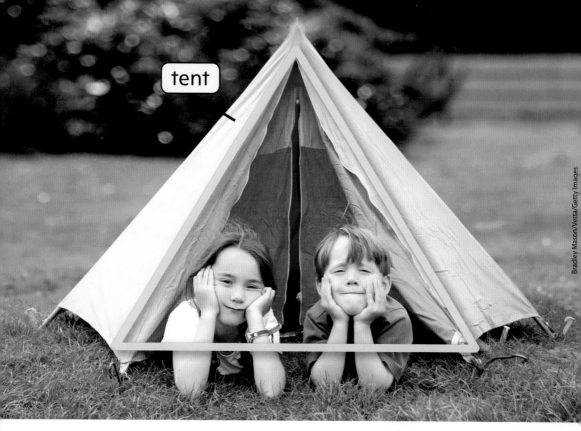
tent

We like the .

tent